CONTENTS

DEDICATION

To the congregation of
First Presbyterian Church, Jackson, Mississippi

And especially to the Reverend Brister H. Ware
Beloved Minister of Pastoral Care
Who has loved us all so well and has helped so many
Standing on Jordan's stormy banks.

Fear Not!

Death and the Afterlife
from a Christian Perspective

Ligon Duncan
with J. Nicholas Reid

CHRISTIAN
FOCUS

Scripture quotations taken from the *Holy Bible, English Standard Version*, copyright © 2001 by Crossway Bibles, a division of Good News Publishers. Used by permission. All rights reserved.

Dr. J. Ligon Duncan III is Senior Pastor of First Presbyterian Church, Jackson, Mississippi. He was moderator of the General Assembly of the Presbyterian Church of America (PCA) in 2004-2005. He is Chairman of the Council on Biblical Manhood and Womanhood, President and Chair of the Council of the Alliance of Confessing Evangelicals.

J. Nicholas Reid is Assistant to Ligon Duncan. He is also the Associate Editor of Reformed Academic Press and is an MDiv candidate at Reformed Theological Seminary, Jackson, Misssissippi. During his time at RTS, he has been both the *Fairbairn Honors Scholar of the Old Testament* and the *Hendricksen Honors Scholar of the New Testament*. Occasionally, Nicholas reviews books for www.reformation21.org, the online magazine for *The Alliance of Confessing Evangelicals*.

ISBN: 978-1-84550-358-1

First published in 2008
Reprinted in 2010
by
Christian Focus Publications Ltd,
Geanies House, Fearn, Tain, Ross-shire,
IV20 1TW, Scotland, Great Britain.
www.christianfocus.com

A CIP catalogue record for this book is available from the British Library.

Cover design by Daniel Van Straaten
Printed by Norhaven, Denmark

FOREWORD

by
Jerry Bridges

Most people, even Christians, live in a state of semi-denial about death. We hesitate to say a dearly loved relative or friend "died." We prefer to say she "passed away" or she "went to be with the Lord." Even unbelievers who assume that everyone ends up in heaven are known to say something such as "he's gone to a better place."

I went to a mortuary to visit the family of a deceased friend. To my amazement, the room where the friend's body was available for viewing was called a "slumber room." I don't know what such a room should be called. But I was struck again by how we use euphemisms to obscure the fact that the person whose body lies in the casket is dead. He is not slumbering; he is dead.

Death, however, is not the final word for either believers or unbelievers. But there is much confusion about what happens to each after death. Two highly successful collegiate football coaches from intensely rival schools died – one of them on the eve of the annual big game between the two schools. During the television broadcast the next day, the TV announcers were commenting on the fact that these two former rival coaches were probably sitting together looking down on the game, presumably from "up in heaven." Quite apart from the fact that neither coach had ever indicated by life or testimony that he would be in heaven, those comments by the TV announcers illustrate the bizarre ideas that many people have of life after death.

We, however, do not have to live in ignorance about life after death for either believers or unbelievers. God's Word, the Bible, tells us everything we need to know. It doesn't tell us everything we might *want* to know, but it tells us everything God wants us to know – which means everything we need to know for our instruction and comfort. And then God has provided ministers to mine His Word for its truths and teach them to the rest of us.

Such a man is J. Ligon Duncan, who is both a scholar and a pastor. With a scholar's mind and a pastor's heart, Dr. Duncan has given to us the excellent book, *Fear Not*, which covers extensively all aspects of death, including what happens to believers immediately after death, the resurrection, the final judgment and then the eternal state. Along the way, he sheds helpful light on several troublesome passages, especially concerning the final Day of Judgment. This is a book to inform and encourage every Christian. All of us will be edified by its pages. It is my pleasure to commend it to every Christian reader.

Jerry Bridges

INTRODUCTION

by
J. Nicholas Reid

Martin Lloyd-Jones once said, "When you are traveling through a bog, you look for solid ground." *Fear Not!* by Dr. J. Ligon Duncan is designed to provide people with greater clarity on the various issues that surround death.

The concern behind this book is less about trying to satisfy curiosity and more about trying to equip people to approach death from a Biblical perspective. Dr. Duncan gave a series of talks on this issue in the spring of 2007. The church hall was packed week after week as people sought to better understand the truths of God's Word. The lady diagnosed with cancer sat attentively with her husband as they tried to find solid ground on which to stand. The bereaved mother sat, as she looked at her one remaining child, curious if she would know in Heaven the little one she lost only a few years before. That couple that we all know and love sat close to one another, as they had been doing for some fifty years at this same church, trying to figure out how they could cope with being soon separated by death. Our people needed to hear the truth proclaimed, and that is just what they got.

As I edited the manuscript and prepared it for publication it soon became apparent that Dr. Duncan's material is practical in its concern, chock full of Scripture, and theologically astute.

Much to her chagrin, we would be remiss if we did not mention Donna Dobbs, Director of Christian Education at First Presbyterian Church, Jackson, who saw the need for a series on death in the life of our church.

We would also like to thank Colin Duriez for his helpful editorial assistance.

Our prayer is that God might use this study to strengthen the hearts of wearied saints as they and their loved ones tread on the verge of Jordan. .

J. Nicholas Reid
In Christ, In Jackson

CHAPTER ONE

What Is Death?

Resolved, to think much, on all occasions of my own dying, and of the common circumstances which attend death.

Jonathan Edwards

Dying to Know

In the wake of certain reading material in the public domain right now, Christians have become increasingly curious about the Bible's answers to various questions relating to death and the afterlife. But it is not just bizarre literature that raises questions about death. Many of the questions raised to me about death over the years have been profoundly personal, specific, and born out of an experience in one's own life and family. Whether death is expected, or considered tragic by all human standards, it raises questions.

The politicians wrote that in this world the only things that are certain are death and taxes. This statement has an element of truth to it. Death is most assuredly a reality for all of us. Every single one of us will deal – if we have not already dealt – with death personally in our own family and in the circle of our closest friends. Likewise, all of us, unless the Lord comes soon, will personally face death. That is why we are looking so intently at death, because death profoundly affects each one of us at the very core of who we are.

Dead Wrong

It should be of no surprise that our world today is confused about death. Many different views about death exist due to the multiple religious beliefs and worldviews in our society. If you believe that there is no God, and that this world evolved from a primitive protein in the explosion of some primary particle, then death is literally meaningless. If you have reduced life to just one sequence of cause and effect, one inexorable chain of events, then after death comes nothing. If you allow that sort of thinking to control the way you approach life and death, then you will approach both fundamentally differently than someone who engages life and death with a biblically informed, Christian worldview.

We do not have to go to non-Christian people, however, to find misunderstandings about death. When we are among our friends and family in the hour of death, we will see many different practical yet confused approaches to death. Some people try to deal with death by denial, pretending that it is just not there.

Several years ago I was able to serve a family during a tragic loss. The sudden death of their family member had taken their breath away. During the course of the family conversation, there was serious discussion among them as to whether they would tell the children in the family that this person had died. I had to spend a lot of time explaining to them the importance of being honest with the children, even as they sought to break the news with sensitivity and care.

Among the bereaved, such a tendency to hide death stems from an attempt to deal with its reality by denial. "We're going to protect the children from death by pretending it's just not here." In the end, such a lapse in judgment exacerbates the problem. The family member that they have just lost is suddenly around no longer, and the child has no clue why. "What happened?" the child might ask. "Was he snatched up into the air? Did I do something wrong to make him not be around me anymore? Doesn't he still love me?" Such uncertainty actually strikes far more terror in the heart of a child than the reality of death, and yet many people have a tendency to deal with it by denial. But such escapism is not a twenty-first century phenomenon; it has been around for a long time.

Louis XV of France demanded that his advisors not use the word "death" around him. But no matter how hard he tried to pretend as if death was not a reality; he still died.

Fear Not!

Despite our denial, the graveyards still fill up. The Bible does not encourage us to deal with death by denial or escapism, but neither does it encourage us to cultivate a stoic attitude towards death.

Very often friends will attempt to comfort you in the hour of death by making diminishing remarks about your loss by finding something positive to say. This is yet another way human beings try to cope with death. Overwhelmed by the emotions associated with death, people sometimes come up with little platitudes to put on a happy face. But we see a glimpse of the goodness of God in that the Bible does not deal with death by denial or pretending like it is no big deal; instead, His Word prepares us by facing the problem of death head on.

All Sin Is Deadly

The Bible paradoxically faces death with utter realism and complete hope in God. We, therefore, must cultivate a biblical way of thinking about death and the last things if we are going to engage them with the right perspective. If we are going to cultivate a Christian perspective about death, then we must begin by trying to understand death itself.

Before death existed in the human world, God was already talking with Adam about it. In Genesis 2:17, the Lord says:

> "But of the tree of the knowledge of good and evil you shall not eat, for in the day that you eat of it you shall surely die."

Death makes its debut in the Bible as a judgment for sin. Sin brings with it, the Apostle Paul will say, its wages, "For the wages of sin is death" (Rom. 6:23a). Before death existed in the human world, God had already explained to Adam: "Adam, rebel, sin against Me, and the consequence, the penalty will be death." At the very outset, the Bible asks us to look at death in judicial terms. Death is not simply the natural end to life; it is God's judgment of sin.

Forrest Gump, that great theologian and philosopher of our age, has popularized a saying that was around long before Winston Groom penned it, "Dyin' is just a part of livin'." Well, I think we all know the point that is being made here, but this saying is not at all a good representation of the biblical view of death. Dying was not part of God's project for Adam living in the garden. Dying was threatened only in the instance of Adam's sin. Sin brought the reality of death into the world. Death, the separation of the body and the soul, is the fruit of sin and the consequence of God's judgment. This, we are told, is the result of Adam's sin:

> "By the sweat of your face you shall eat bread, till you return
> to the ground, for out of it you were taken; for you are dust
> and to dust you shall return." (Gen. 3:19)

In fulfillment of the warning given to Adam in Genesis 2:17, God pronounces a curse after he rebels, which results in Adam and Eve being driven out of the Garden of Eden.

Sin brings about separation, and there are two separations that occur in Genesis 3. First of all, Adam and Eve are separated from God (Gen. 3:23). Adam and Eve can no longer stay in the garden. But what does this judgment mean? Adam and Eve being driven out of the garden is a picture of the loss of life.

Genesis 3:8 says: "And they heard the sound of the LORD God walking in the garden in the cool of the day…." How many of you have ever heard the sound of God walking in the garden? Me neither! The only people in the history of this world who knew what it sounds like for God to walk in the garden with them decided to listen to a serpent, rather than to love God. We lost that privilege at the Fall.

God walking in the garden in Genesis 3 is a picture of the life, communion, fellowship, and enjoyment of the living God that had been given to Adam and Eve. But in Genesis 3:24, Adam and Eve are driven out of the garden as a consequence of their sin. Separation has occurred, and in being separated from God, they are separated from life – life as it was intended to be. God intended us to enjoy life, but man forfeited all true life, all true joy, all true peace by sinning against God.

That is why Jesus says, "I came to give life, and that abundantly." The biblical concept of life is not having an abundance of things in this world; instead, abundant life is communing and fellowshipping with the living God. By sinning against God, Adam and Eve lost the privilege of abundant life for the whole world, but Jesus Christ came into this world in order to regain that privilege for a multitude of men and women, boys and girls, a multitude that no man can number, from every tribe, tongue, people, and nation. What Adam lost, Jesus lived and died and rose from the dead to give. Death must be contemplated in terms of the just judgment of God on sin.

Secondly, sin caused a separation in us. The separation of the body and soul is a sign of the physical separation from God that is brought about by physical death – a separation that will be deepened after death for those who leave this world without Christ.

The Bible – from beginning to end – views death as "the last enemy"; not because this life is the thing that we treasure above everything else, but because our supreme treasure – above all other things – is God, and death is the judgment that comes against those who have rebelled against God and lost the right to life and communion with Him. The Christian view of death is radically different from an unbeliever's view of it because the Christian desires more than anything to have communion with God. One old saint put it this way:

As a believer's life is very different from an unbeliever's life, so also a believer's death is very different from an unbeliever's death. The unbeliever prefers Heaven over Hell;

the believer prefers Heaven over this earth. The unbeliever prefers Heaven only over Hell because he cannot imagine anything more blessed than this life. The believer prefers Heaven over earth, because the believer cannot imagine anything more blessed than life with God.

The believer and unbeliever look at death dramatically differently, because death is not the end for the believer. The thing that the believer longs for more than anything else is communion with the living God, but death is the visible picture of the just judgment of God against all those who have fallen into sin – sinners have no right to enjoy communion with the living God. So death and the dissolution of the body and spirit is a picture of spiritual separation from God.

The Paradox of Death

There is something very strange about the way the Bible speaks about death. It pictures death as an enemy, and yet still speaks of death in comforting terms to believers.

All the way back in Genesis 49, Israel could describe his death as being "gathered to his people." In 2 Kings 22:20, God said to Hezekiah that he was going to be "gathered to" his "grave in peace." In Psalm 116:15, we're told that death is precious – "precious in the sight of the LORD is the death of his saints." In Luke 16:22, Jesus refers to death as being "carried by the angels to Abraham's side." In Luke 23:43, He can speak to a thief on the cross in terms of being with Him, "Today you will be with me in Paradise." In John 14:2, Jesus can describe the death of His disciples in terms of going to the many mansions, which He has prepared for them. In 2 Corinthians 5:8, we are told that death is like being "at home with the Lord." In Philippians 1:21, death is called "gain." In Philippians 1:23, death is called "far better." And in 1 Thessalonians 4:13, the believer's death is described as those who have fallen asleep. What beautiful pictures of death!

On the one hand, death is the last enemy. Believers, too, are sinners, and so unless the Lord comes soon, we will all taste death. The Christian views death as an enemy; it is not a natural part of life. Death is actually the way things were never intended to be. Death is a judgment of God against sin. Death is the most unnatural thing in this world. But on the other hand, death has become for the believer an entrance into glory.

The Transformation of Death

But how was death transformed? How is the believer not only able to view death as the last enemy, but also as his entrance into glory? The fifth of seven benedictions that John the apostle pronounces in the Book of Revelation, says:

Blessed and holy is the one who shares in the first resurrection! Over such the second death has no power,

> but they will be priests of God and of Christ, and they will
> reign with him for a thousand years. (Rev. 20:6)

Death was transformed for the believer when God sent His Son into this world and placed Him on the cross. Jesus Christ experienced the second death on behalf of His people – second death is biblical shorthand for the eternal judgment and punishment that awaits those who have not trusted in the Lord Jesus Christ. After the believer experiences the first death, he does not taste the second death. For the Christian, death is no longer a precursor to the final judgment and separation of God; instead, death is now transformed to the portal into the presence of God.

When Adam and Eve were kicked out of the garden, angels were placed on guard to keep them from returning to Eden. The angelic guard was something that Adam and Eve could not pass through. They were unable to enter into the presence of God; they were cut off from the Living God. Likewise, death is this thing that is mightier than we, and there is no way that we can pass through it unscathed in our own strength. Death is too deadly for us. But when Jesus Christ conquered death and robbed it of its sting, He enabled every believer to pass through death – the last enemy – into glory. Doug Kelly, Professor of Systematic Theology at Reformed Theological Seminary Charlotte, put it this way, "When death took on Jesus, it bit off more than it could chew." Since Jesus experienced the second death on behalf of His people, our whole view of death is transformed.

When death catches us by surprise, we can be tempted to think that God does not understand what we are feeling and experiencing. But when God sent Jesus into this world, the Father knew that he was sending His Son to die. And not only would He have to die, but He would have to experience the second death that none of you who have trusted in Christ will ever experience. So when you are looking at the cold body of a loved one who has been taken from you, and you are tempted to think, "Lord, You do not understand what I am feeling," it is vital for you to know that your heavenly Father understands things about death that you cannot conceive. His Son, the Lord Jesus Christ, experienced a death that neither you nor anyone else who trusts in Him will ever experience. This is what the Apostle Paul means when he says in Romans 8:32, "He who did not spare his own Son but gave him up for us all, how will he not also with him graciously give us all things?" The Father gave His Son to walk into not only the first death, but the second death, in our place, so that we would never feel the full force of what death was intended to be – eternal separation from a good and loving God on account of our rebellion. This truth radically transforms the way a believer looks at death.

First of all, we can never, ever, approach death – no matter how surprising, shocking, crushing, and tragic it may be in our experience – with a hint of a suspicion that our heavenly Father does not understand what we are going through. If you have lost a child, you can take comfort that your heavenly Father knows what it is like to lose a child. He knows what it is like not only to lose a child, but to give a child to be lost for you. It is supremely unwise to look up into His loving eyes and say, "My Father, You don't know what I'm going through," because He can look right back at you and say, "Child, you cannot fathom what I have gone through for you." Although there are a thousand mysteries in death, and it is precisely that fear of the unknown – even among believers – that unsettles us from time to time, Jesus Christ radically changes the way a Christian looks at death. There is nothing unknown about death to God; in fact, God created death as judgment, and His own Son experienced the judgment of death in the place of His people. There is nothing about death that He does not understand, and so you can trust Him even in your darkest hour. That is why David can say in Psalm 23:4, "Even though I walk through the valley of the shadow of death, I will fear no evil, for you are with me; your rod and your staff, they comfort me." David did not know precisely what was waiting for him in the valley of the shadow of death, but his God did, and that is all that matters.

As Christians, we understand death to be the last enemy, but we also understand that Christ has conquered that last enemy by experiencing the second death on our behalf, so that when we experience the first death – the separation of soul and body – we do so now without the dread of God's righteous judgment, but as the beginning of God giving to us that which He created us for in the first place: life, and that abundantly!

Over and over the Bible speaks of the Christian life in terms of dying. Paul says, "I die daily." Jesus speaks of "laying down His life that you might have life." That is why every Christian should study death, and every minister worth his salt wants not only to prepare you for purpose in this life, but wants to prepare you for death, as well. The moment of a Christian's death is his passageway into glory, and so we must be prepared for that moment whenever it may come. This means that we must teach our children to understand what death is and to approach it with a biblical understanding: not in denial or escapism; not in stoic, emotionless detachment; but in realism and in hope, recognizing what death is, but also recognizing what Jesus's death has done to death for all who trust in Christ.

In many ways, this is the most difficult lesson that we have to learn about death, but it lays the foundation for all the encouragement that we are going to receive as we consider what happens to the believer after death, what happens when Christ returns, what happens for the believer in the Day of Judgment, and what heaven is and how we prepare for it.

Fear Not!

In order to find comfort as we experience loss, we must begin with understanding death, because this is the wages of sin; but in Christ, through free grace, we have been given a gift from God. This gift – the Apostle Paul says in the very same verse that he announces that the wages of sin is death – is eternal life in communion with our holy, perfect, ever-blessed, altogether lovely Triune God. The first death – my death, your death – is the passageway to eternal *life* for all who trust in Jesus.

Heavenly Father, we ask that You would help us to think about death Christian-ly; to be informed by the Bible in our understanding of it; and so to be transformed in the way that we cope with death in our own lives and in the losses that we experience amongst friends and family. Help us to be an encouragement to one another, speaking to one another in psalms and hymns and spiritual songs, and reminding one another of the glory of what Jesus has done for us, that we might never taste the second death. These things we ask in Jesus's name. Amen.

CHAPTER TWO

What Happens After Death?

Bereave me of the satisfaction of Christ, and I am bereaved.
If He fulfilled not justice, I must. If He underwent not wrath,
I must unto eternity. O, rob me not of my only pearl.

John Owen

Guilt, Meaning, and Death

Every single human being has to deal with three problems in
life: the problems of guilt, meaning, and death.

First, every human being, no matter how seared his or her
conscience may be, from time to time feels the pangs of guilt,
and asks the question, "In light of my guilt (that is, in light
of my own self-recognition that I have done wrong), how
can I be put right? How can my guilt be dealt with? How
can my wrong-doing be resolved in such a way that I am
made right, that I'm put right with God and others?" Every
human being wrestles with the issue of guilt.

Secondly, every human being also wrestles with the issue
of meaning. Even professors who tell their college freshmen
that there is – ultimately speaking – no meaning to this life

know that such a philosophy does not work. Human beings aren't built to survive that way. If there were no meaning in this life, then human beings would not be able to carry on. No one truly lives as if everything is meaningless.

Thirdly, every human being also wrestles with the question of death. "What happens when I die? What is death? What is beyond this life? How do I address the fear of that transition?" Only Christianity, only the Bible, only Christ, only the gospel can give you a sufficient answer to those three questions. My friends, I would love to discuss all three of these in detail with you, but my job at present is to think about the third one. How does the Bible speak of death? And what does the Bible say happens after death?

The Believer's Death

The Bible teaches that God has for us in the gospel of Jesus Christ not only blessings here in this life, but blessings after this life is done. The apostle Paul says emphatically, "If in this life only we have hoped in Christ, we are of all people most to be pitied" (1 Cor. 15:19). "If the dead are not raised, 'Let us eat and drink, for tomorrow we die'" (v. 32b). Now that is not a charlatan on the street corner saying this; it is the apostle Paul. He is not simply trusting in Christ so that this life might be more full or more prosperous; instead, he is trusting in Christ for this life and forevermore, for this life and eternity, for this life and the life to come. Christian hope is a hope that not only controls our present living, but also our anticipation of what will come to be beyond this life.

The Westminster Shorter Catechism 37 is instructive here. "What benefits do believers receive from Christ at death?"

> The souls of believers are at their death made perfect in holiness, and do immediately pass into glory; and their bodies, being still united to Christ, do rest in their graves till the resurrection.

Thomas Vincent, who wrote an early commentary on *The Shorter Catechism,* says that this answer teaches that the benefits of believers at death are twofold: first in regard to their souls, and second in regard to their bodies.

What happens to believers the second we shuffle off this mortal coil? What happens to believers the nanosecond our final breath has left our bodies and our brains and hearts fail us? What happens instantaneously for the believer at death?

Before we look more intently at the blessings that belong to all believers in death, we must realize that these blessings – as comforting as they may be – do not mean that death is easy for the believer. The great English Baptist minister, William Kiffin, who believed all the promises that we are about to study, wrote these words when his wife died:

> It pleased the Lord to take to Himself my dear and faithful wife, with whom I have lived nearly 42 years, whose tenderness to me and faithfulness to God were such as cannot

by me be expressed, as she continually sympathized with me in all my afflictions. I can truly say that I never heard her utter the least discontent under all the various providences that attended either me or her. She eyed the hand of God in all our sorrows, and so constantly encouraged me in the ways of God. Her death was the greatest sorrow to me that I ever met in the Lord.

My friends, I want you to understand that those are the words of a Christian, and the Lord would not rebuke William Kippen for penning them. Although the Lord through the apostle Paul explicitly says to believers, "But we do not want you to be uninformed, brothers, about those who are asleep, that you may not grieve as others do who have no hope" (1 Thess. 4:13), the Lord does *not* say to believers, "Do not grieve." Instead, he says, "You do not grieve as those without hope."

Christian grief has mingled with it an inextinguishable, inexhaustible, irrepressible hope, the type of hope that enabled Job to say, "Though he slay me, I will hope in him..." (Job 13:15). In the face of death, a Christian does not approach death with stoic indifference or emotionless detachment because of the hope that is theirs in God. Do not think for a second that we are commending a stoic approach to death – instead, we are commending an approach that is filled with the comfort of God because of the certainty of His promises, even in the midst of the difficulty of it all.

Definitive Difference

The way a believer approaches death is fundamentally different from that of an unbeliever. Thomas Boston once said:

> All men must die, but as men's lives are very different, so their account in death is, also. To an ungodly man, death is loss, the greatest loss; but to a believer, it is gain, the greatest gain.

Why is that? Why is death totally different for the believer and for the unbeliever? Richard Baxter helpfully elaborates on this point:

> There is a great deal of difference between the desires of Heaven in a sanctified man and in an unsanctified one. The believer prizes Heaven above earth, and had rather be with God than here, though death stands in the way and may possibly have harder thoughts from him. But for the ungodly, there is nothing that seems more desirable than this world, and therefore he only chooses Heaven over Hell, but not over earth; and therefore shall not have it upon such a choice.

Baxter is saying that nobody in his right mind would choose Hell. If they are asked, then they'll always say, "Oh, yes, heaven over hell, please!" In contrast, the mark of a Christian approaching death is a desire for heaven over earth, heaven over this life. The Christian desires Jesus over the things that are most precious in this world, and not simply an existence that is more attractive than the torments of an eternity in Hell.

In Christ Alone

In the catechism passage we mentioned earlier, we learn of four blessings that belong to believers even in the valley of the shadow of death. These blessings are why the death of a believer is not only a day of mourning, but also one of triumph. We are especially comforted upon the deaths of believers because they have trusted in Christ alone for salvation, as He is freely offered in the gospel. Therefore, as we contemplate their deaths, whoever they may be, we can rest assured that they have received these four things immediately upon dying.

1. When believers die, they are immediately with Christ, whom they prize more than all things.

This is the *greatest blessing* of the believer at death. Everything else pales in comparison with this one truth. In 2 Corinthians 5:8, the Apostle Paul is speaking of himself and by extension to all believers saying: "Yes, we are of good courage, and we would rather be away from the body and at home with the Lord." For the Christian to be absent from this body – this is Paul's way of speaking of death – is to be at home with the Lord. The apostle Paul anticipates immediately being with the Lord when he dies. Since the believer prizes Christ more than anything else, this is his most cherished blessing. Samuel Rutherford once said, "I am so in love with His love that if He were not in Heaven, I would not want to go there." Rutherford longed to be with Him because he prized Christ and treasured His love for him above all.

Every gospel minister knows that you were made for joy, but the problem is that this world tries to trick you into thinking that you can find it apart from the Lord Jesus Christ. So, the gospel minister fights for your joy, not that you will take joy in the passing, trivial things of this world, but so that you will rejoice and delight in Christ alone. The things of this world need to fade in their value before your eyes. You must learn to treasure and long for Christ, and long to be with Him more than anything else.

The apostle Paul is assuring us that for the believer to be absent from the body is to be immediately with the Lord. You ask me, "Where is that going to be?" I do not know. It does not matter. All I need to know is this: to be absent from the body is to be present with the Lord. Where is the Lord? He is at the right hand of God. Where is the right hand of God? I do not know, but my Lord is there, and that is all that matters. I am to be with Him. I am to be present with the One for whom my soul longs.

For the believer, Christ is more precious than husband or wife, than parents or children, than riches, than fame, than power, than ambition, than influence, than success, than pleasure. He is more valuable than anything. It is no wonder Job could say, "Though he slay me, I will hope in him..." (Job 13:15), because he himself would later say, "And after my skin has been thus destroyed, yet in my flesh I shall see God, whom I shall see for myself, and my eyes shall behold, and not another" (Job 19:26-27). Job's longing was to be present with God, which is the first and greatest blessing that believers receive. We are with Christ. Paul says, "Yes, we are of good courage, and we would rather be away from the body and at home with the Lord" (2 Cor. 5:8).

2. *When believers die, they are immediately perfected in holiness.*
The author of Hebrews speaks of *the spirits of the righteous made perfect*, and he is emphasizing that those of us who have come to Christ are part of this perfected company of believers (Heb. 12:22-24). Immediately upon our death, we enter into the presence of God and are perfected; perfected in holiness, made perfect in godliness, freed from sin, and made in the likeness of Christ.

The book of Revelation frequently describes the saints who have gone before us – that is, believers who have died in Jesus Christ and are waiting for the day of resurrection – as perfected; no longer committing sin, no longer struggling with the temptations that result because of indwelling sin, and freed completely from the very possibility of sin. If you are like me, this thought is extremely comforting, because a thousand times a day my heart is tempted to be disloyal to God. My heart is tempted to love things that I ought not to love and so betray my Lord and God. But, oh, to be in a place where I never again, *never again*, have the slightest tinge of temptation to defect from loving loyalty and blessed service to my Savior. That is a precious thought: made perfect in holiness, with our minds illumined and our wills made perfectly upright, resulting in our actions matching perfectly God's good will. The thought of such bliss and rest is overwhelming.

The transition of death can be daunting, even to a believer. But even as daunting as death may be for the believer, it also means a final cessation of that internal warfare against sin, which is a reality that is beyond our imagining. I have no idea what it is like to live with a heart that is wholly given over to my God. I have not lived one second with that kind of heart. But one day I will.

If you believe in the Lord Jesus Christ as He is offered in the gospel, then at death the warfare is over. The battle is done. Your heart becomes wholly and solely His. Instantaneously in the moment of death, Satan can never ever again get his hook in your heart and use something in you to pull you away from your Lord, because you will be perfected in holiness.

3. When believers die, they pass immediately into glory.

In Philippians 1:23, the apostle Paul says that he desires to depart and be with Christ, for that is much better. Why is it much better? Death is better because we pass into glory with

Jesus Christ. We pass into a glorious place. We are welcomed into the Father's house (John 14:2). As the apostle Paul said in 2 Corinthians 5:8, when we are absent from the body, we are at home with the Lord. That concept should certainly change the way you look at death.

I can remember thinking on numerous occasions during the years that I spent studying in St. Louis, Missouri, and then in Edinburgh, Scotland, "If I can just get home and be with my family, everything will be all right." I can remember driving down the interstate or flying on a plane across the ocean thinking the same. Well, Paul said, in effect, "Let me tell you what happens when you die. The minute you pass into death, you come home." I love the way Isaac Watts paraphrases the end of Psalm 23:

> Here would we find a settled rest,
> While others go and come;
> Not like a stranger or a guest,
> But like a child at home.

The minute death comes, you are safe at home; safe in the Father's arms; safe with your older brother, Jesus Christ, who shed His blood so that you could come home. Immediately!

One of the thieves on the cross who had been mocking Jesus earlier in the day – as one of the gospel writers tells us – was convicted by what he saw and heard from Jesus Christ. He began to rebuke the other thief, saying, "Do you not fear

God, since you are under the same sentence of condemnation?" At one point the thief says to Jesus, "Jesus, remember me when you come into your kingdom." And then Jesus replies, "Today you will be with me in Paradise" (Luke 23). Like a child going home, the thief passed into glory, to the Father's house. Believers immediately enter into that place, into that society, into that state, a truth we must never forget.

I knew a couple that lost their first son at the age of four through a recurrence of cancer. I am still awe struck by the way they cared for that child! They held and nurtured him continuously as his life slipped away. I said to the mother at one point, "Doreen, you understand that Michael is going to go instantaneously from your arms to the arms of Jesus; and for him on the other side, it won't seem like there's been any separation from you. Death will be like walking through a portal, to where his Savior is waiting, and one day you will go to be with him. Now for you, how many years it will be, I don't know. Your heart will be empty as you wait. As for him, he'll look around and not only will his God be there, his Savior will be there, but one day you too will be there."[1]

4. *When believers die, their bodies remain united to Christ, resting in the grave, awaiting the resurrection.*
The Thessalonians had been upset by someone who had been teaching in their midst that there is uncertainty about

what happens to believers who die before Jesus returns. The Thessalonians knew that Jesus would come again, and they were certain that if they were alive when he came, they would be with the Lord, but they were not certain about their relatives who had died in Christ before them. So, the apostle Paul pastorally wanted to assure them, "But we do not want you to be uninformed, brothers, about those who are asleep, that you may not grieve as others do who have no hope" (1 Thess. 4:13).

Paul did not even say this in terms of the imperative. He does not even say to Thessalonians, "Do not grieve as those who have no hope!" Instead he says, in effect, "It is my pastoral concern for you that you do not grieve as those who have no hope."

God comforts his people by saying: "If we believe that Jesus died and rose again, even so God will bring with Him those who have fallen asleep in Jesus." What a beautiful way to describe a believer's death, "Fallen asleep in Jesus." This concept is so comforting that our Lutheran friends often put that on the gravestones of departed saints: "Asleep in Jesus." This metaphor of sleep that Paul employs takes the entire sting out of death. Death is not a place of darkness and uncertainty; it is a place of repose and rest where Jesus Himself in the hour of death cradles and cares for the believer. But Paul goes on to say in 1 Thessalonians 4:13-18, to paraphrase: "For this we declare to you by a word from the Lord, that we who are alive, who are left until the coming of the Lord, will not precede those who have fallen asleep."

In other words, we are not in a position that is better than those who have already died in Christ. In fact, when Jesus returns, the dead in the Lord will rise first, then we who remain alive shall be caught up together with them in the clouds to meet the Lord in the air, and thus we shall always be with the Lord. The apostle Paul is stressing that God will so care for the bodies of the deceased that on the last day their bodies will be transformed, united with their spirits, and will even go before us as we are caught up to be with the Lord.

Your loved ones, who have died resting and trusting in Jesus Christ alone for salvation as He is offered in the gospel, are more alive now than they have ever been because they are united to Christ. Clement Graham's note on the flowers that he placed on the casket at his wife's funeral read: "You are alive in Christ, and forever in my heart."

At Douglas McMillan's[2] funeral, Donald Macleod[3] said that it is hard for us to contemplate this big, loving, energetic man dead and immobilized, without energy, vigor, life, force and activity; and then he reminded everyone, on the basis of 1 Thessalonians 4, that Douglas is more alive, more vigorous, more energetic, more active than he has ever been before. He has been perfected. The metaphor of "asleep in Jesus" is not a metaphor of inactivity; it is a metaphor of rest. It reminds us that at the end of this long struggle comes rest.

Fear Not!

Death for the Unbeliever

Although believers are united to Christ and are at rest when they die, the Bible also teaches that unbelievers are eternally separated from Christ. Unbelievers are sealed in their imperfection and are in a state of condemnation, permanently separated from Christ, never again to know peace and rest.

John Macleod, who was voted the Scottish Journalist of the Year twice, had the temerity as a columnist for *The Glasgow Herald*, the largest secular newspaper in Scotland, to write an article on Hell, which he called "Between Satan's Spandau and a Hard Place." In this fascinating article, he wrote:

> There are few of us who care to acknowledge our through-and-through depravity, and there can be no-one reading this column who has never been bereaved. To face the possibility of Hell as our final end is at present enough; to realize that many – any – of our loved ones may be there already is to know true horror.
>
> Now, your intrepid columnist is a buoyant and cheerful fellow, and nothing would delight him more than to be able to assure his readers, that Hell is a medieval fiction. But he cannot.
>
> Hell flows logically from the teaching of Scripture. The terrible end that awaits the ungodly is stressed from Genesis to Revelation, as much a part of the New Testament teaching as the Old. Indeed, Jesus in the Gospels refers more often to Hell than anyone else in the Bible. He believes in it

in sober earnest, after all, He created it. For Hell is not the place of Satan's kingdom, it is the place of Satan's banishment by the Lord. Hell will be Satan's Sandau.

The doctrine of Hell necessarily flows from the founding precepts of Christianity. Man – oh, all right, Maria Fyfe, humankind; but Man is quicker – has been made in the image of God. He is above all other creatures, he has self-awareness, self-knowledge, the capacity to relate, to create, to dream. And he is immortal. The soul – the "think" – must live forever. It cannot cease to be, for it is of God. In our hearts we all know that death is unnatural, the change appalling, the grave obscene.

But when man has rejected God in this world – when he has gone his own way, when he has rejected the moral law – what then? The logic of God precludes eternal fellowship with such a being, who has despised His law and defied His will. And when the Gospel itself is spurned, and the way of Christ's atonement, ignored what can there be at the last for such a man but to grant his heart's desire?"[4]

John Macleod is saying that since you want none of God here, God will give you what you want. There will be no one in hell who wants to be in heaven; they will all want to be out of hell, but none will truly desire to be in heaven. Jesus, in Matthew 8:12, says that it's a place of weeping, but it is also a place of gnashing of teeth. When you get mad and you just want to hit somebody, and your teeth just start clenching down, you are gnashing your teeth. In Hell, people are gnashing their teeth at God! There is no repentance there. There is no one saying, "I wish I were with You, God." There is no one in hell who wants to be in heaven. They have repudiated God in this life, and so they forgo Him forever.

The Greeks had a saying that went like this: "Whom the gods would destroy, they answer their prayers." The point is that sometimes we want things that will kill us, and sometimes we get them. To those who want to forego God in this life, God says to them, "Fine."

John Macleod goes on to say:

I have never doubted the reality of such a place, but Hades of deep and lasting darkness. But I have never thought of it in popular terms, as a rather nasty boiler room run by wee men in red tights. Hell is ultimately a negative, a place of nothing but anguish: it is a place without God, and without anything of God, without light, without warmth, without friendship, without peace. No racks, no pincers, no claws: only the fires of an awakened conscience and a burning thirst of a frustrated ego.

The wicked ones of history: they will be there. The killers and the exploiters; they will be there. Libertines and gossips, rapists and drunkards, they will be there. Those whose gods were Sex, or Money, or Ambition, or Power, they will be there, Catholics, Baptists, Free Presbyterians ... if their only faith was their religiosity, who had nothing for eternity but denominational adherence – they will be there. And in the darkest, thickest corner of all: the nice ministers, the jolly vicars: the benevolent bishops, who told their people it was

Heaven for all, and that love is all that matters and that they should really join the Constitutional Convention.

This I believe. And I believe, too, that there is only one escape: by flight to Christ and faith in His finished work, living in His service, but never looking to such toils for my salvation. But there is the final paradox: to believe in this latter end of all things, and to live and walk in a world that must one day melt in fervent heat – to walk among the living dead, with my bright smile and polite talk, and never to challenge, and never to warn."[5]

What happens after death for those who do not rest and trust in Jesus Christ? They get no Christ, which means no enjoyment, no fellowship, and no love. They get eternal separation from the Lord Jesus Christ. It is the most solemn thing possible.

In my sinful moments – and I stress my *sinful* moments, because every true believer knows that God is good – there is no doctrine that I want to be untrue more than the reality of hell. I wish I could say that this doctrine is not true. But *hell is the fairest reality in this world*.

If you want unfairness, if you want discrimination, I can give you that. That is called heaven by grace. Heaven by grace is the most unfair doctrine imaginable. Sinners deserving condemnation get heaven forever because the One who was without sin became sin for their reconciliation. That is unfair, but hell is the fairest doctrine in the world. In hell, you not only get what you want, you get what you deserve. In hell,

Fear Not!

you are paid your wages. In hell, you reap what you have sown. It is the fairest doctrine in the world. Heaven, that is unfair. A sinner enjoying Christ for all eternity is unfair.

Give me unfair! I will take heaven by grace.

Lord, it is so important that we understand what You tell us about what happens after death, because so many people live as if this life is all that counts, all that matters, all there is. And we know, O God, that in many ways this life is but a staging ground for a much longer enduring reality, but an enduring reality that has two and only two destinations: everlasting joy, satisfaction and fulfillment in Christ, or everlasting sorrow, frustration, and un-fulfillment without Him. Surely there could be nothing more solemn than for human beings created in the image of God to consider our end. Give us wisdom as we do this to think Your thoughts after You, according to Your Word. In Jesus's name we pray. Amen.

CHAPTER THREE

What Happens When Christ Returns?
The Resurrection of Christ and the Resurrection of the Body

In the death of Christ, we see God's condemnation of sin, but in the resurrection, we see God's acquittal of sinners.

Herman Ridderbos

Does the resurrection really matter, or is it merely a secondary issue of the Christian faith? After all, there were many in Jesus's day and in the days of Paul that thought there was no such thing as a resurrection. So is the resurrection really a matter of importance? Do we really have to understand the resurrection if we are going to understand death?

The Importance of the Resurrection
In Corinthians 15, Paul gives four reasons why the resurrection is of the utmost importance as he corrects the church at Corinth's misunderstandings. The apostle Paul clearly shows that the resurrection is anything but a secondary issue in this life or in the life to come.

Fear Not!

1. The resurrection is part of the gospel and necessary for our salvation (1-2).

In verses 1 and 2, Paul makes it clear that the resurrection is part of the gospel, and therefore it is necessary for salvation. As far as the apostle Paul is concerned, the physical, bodily resurrection is an indispensable element of our faith.[6] Paul says that if we are not raised again in the flesh, then we are of all people most miserable. Paul is deadly serious about the bodily resurrection, not only Christ's resurrection, but of the believer's resurrection too.

The resurrection is an essential part of the gospel, and so you cannot have one without the other. There is no gospel apart from bodily resurrection.

> Now I would remind you, brothers, of the gospel I preach-
> ed to you, which you received, in which you stand, and
> by which you are being saved, if you hold fast to the
> word I preached to you – unless you believed in vain.
> (1 Cor. 15:1-2)

The message that Paul preached was of first importance – the message by which we are saved. Part of this infinitely important message is that Christ was raised on the third day, according to the Scriptures (1 Corinthians 15:4). Thus, the apostle Paul in effect is saying, "Believers should believe in the resurrection because it is part of the gospel and thus necessary for our salvation."

2. The resurrection was not a doctrine Paul made up; instead, he "received" it just as we should.

Secondly, Paul makes it clear to us that he did not invent the doctrine of the resurrection of Christ. Instead, he *received* the doctrine of the resurrection from the Lord Jesus Christ. Verses 3 and 4 say:

> For I delivered to you as of first importance what I also received: that Christ died for our sins in accordance with the Scriptures, that he was buried, that he was raised on the third day in accordance with the Scriptures.

The apostle Paul is saying in effect to these Corinthian Christians and to the church through the ages, "I am not the originator of the Christian idea of the resurrection of Jesus Christ. The doctrine of the resurrection was delivered to me, and I am delivering it to you. I received it firsthand when I became a Christian."

When the apostle Paul was converted, the resurrected Jesus Christ met him on the road to Damascus. From this time on he did not need complex arguments to convince him about the reality of the resurrection of Christ.[7]

Paul was a firm believer in that resurrection, and so he is stressing, "Look, I didn't invent this. This was something I received and then delivered to you." The apostle wants to make sure that Christians know that the resurrection is not something he made up; instead, he received it from the Lord Jesus Christ. Therefore, we should receive it as well.

3. The resurrection is copiously attested as an historical event by people of the highest integrity.

Thirdly, Paul goes out of his way to point out that the resurrection is copiously attested as an historical event by people of the highest integrity (1 Cor. 15:5-10). He names people who had personally seen the resurrected Christ, many of whom were known to the Corinthians.

Paul not only points out that Jesus appeared to Cephas (Peter), to James, and to all the rest of the apostles, but he also says that Jesus appeared to more than five hundred brothers at one time, "most of whom are still alive, though some have fallen asleep" (v. 6). Do you realize what an astounding claim that is? If Paul were lying, he was giving five hundred people – most of whom were still alive – the opportunity to refute his assertion that Jesus had been resurrected. In other words, "Corinthians, most of these five hundred that He appeared to are still alive. Ask them if you do not believe me." Paul is in effect saying, "Look, Corinthians. This is not mere wishful thinking. This is not the crazy idea of one man, or two men, or even three. This is something copiously attested to by people of integrity."

4. The resurrection is part of the core teaching of the apostles and the apostolic church.

Fourthly, in verse 11, Paul says that this resurrection is part of the core teaching of the apostles, and thus characterizes any church that is truly apostolic. When Paul uses the word, *apostolic*, he means a church that is in accord with the teaching of the apostles. Paul knows that the apostles' teaching is normative for Christians. This is a concept that a number of Christians – especially who have lived in the English-speaking world over the last two hundred years – could well afford to learn more about. This is because there are a lot of Christians, even professors of theology and ministers, who think that they have the right to invent Christianity in their own imaginations, to essentially make it up as they go along. But as far as the apostle Paul is concerned, a truly Christian church follows the teachings of the apostles. In verse 11, he says, "Whether then it was I or they, so we preach and so you believed." He is essentially saying, "I, and all the apostles, preached the resurrection – the physical, bodily resurrection – of Jesus Christ, and we have preached it as essential to the gospel of grace." So the resurrection is part of the core teaching of the apostles and any truly apostolic church.

The Implications of the Resurrection

Paul makes this argument as to why we ought to believe the resurrection, but what difference does that make?

In 1 Corinthians 15:12ff, Romans, and in other places throughout his writings, Paul tells us why the resurrection is so vitally important. It would be beyond the scope of this present work to exhaustively deal with each of the implications Paul offers in his letters, so I will limit myself to five crucial implications of the resurrection.

1. Paul stresses that the resurrection bears witness to the veracity or truthfulness of the claims made by the church regarding the person and work of Christ.

In other words, the resurrection vindicates the claims that the church has made about who Jesus is, what He came to do, and what he has accomplished in His life, ministry, and death. The resurrection validates the claims that the church in its preaching makes about the person and work of Christ.

In Romans 1, Paul says that Jesus was declared to be the Son of God with power "by his resurrection from the dead." Jesus was publicly declared and vindicated as the Son of God by the resurrection.

Jesus Himself also explicitly declared that He is the Son of God, and the apostles attested to this reality. When the disciples were at Caesarea Philippi talking amongst themselves about what people were saying about Jesus, He asks them, "So, what are people saying about me?" And the disciples reply something like this, "Well, Lord, some of them say You are John the Baptist, risen again from the dead. Some people say that You are Elijah." Then Jesus says, "Well, I want to know who you think I am." Peter blurts out, in typical Peter fashion, "You are the Christ, the Son of the living God" (Matt. 16:16). Jesus responds by saying, "Blessed are you,

Simon Bar-Jonah! For flesh and blood has not revealed this to you, but my Father who is in heaven" (Matt.16:17).

The disciples recognized the true nature of Jesus, and Jesus Himself declared that He was the Son of God, but the resurrection was a demonstration of His nature. Death could not hold Him, and His resurrection vindicates His claim to be the very Son of God. So the resurrection is evidential. It is part of the proof of Jesus's person and the effectiveness of His atoning work. The resurrection distinguishes Jesus from all the other leaders of the world's religions, and naturally gives us great confidence to receive His teaching.

2. The apostle Paul says the resurrection is important because it is at the heart of the apostolic preaching and connected to the gospel of redemption and justification.

"Jesus our Lord ... was delivered up for our trespasses and raised for our justification." (Rom. 4:24-25). The apostle Paul is saying that our justification – our being declared right with God, forgiven of our sins, and accepted as righteous in God's sight not for anything in us, but for Jesus Christ's blood alone – is something that Christ's resurrection has accomplished. He was raised for our justification, so the resurrection is part and parcel of the gospel, the good news.

The gospel preached by the apostles included testimony to the resurrection as one of its characteristic features. If you do a study of the preaching of the apostles in Romans,

Fear Not!

Acts, 1 Corinthians, and in other places, you will find that the resurrection of Jesus Christ is repeatedly emphasized. The resurrection gives assurance to us that Christ's work is complete, and our redemption is accomplished.

3. The resurrection is the source of the new life of the believer, and it is the fountainhead of our growing in grace and godliness, or what theologians call sanctification.

> We were buried therefore with him by baptism into death, in order that, just as Christ was raised from the dead by the glory of the Father, we too might walk in newness of life. (Rom. 6:4)

We have been raised with Christ to walk in newness of life. Christ's resurrection is the source of the Christian life from beginning to end. The resurrection gives new life to the believer and is the very fountainhead of our growth in grace and godly living.

4. The resurrection is the source, example, and guarantee of our future resurrection.

> If the Spirit of him who raised Jesus from the dead dwells in you, he who raised Christ Jesus from the dead will also give life to your mortal bodies through his Spirit who dwells in you. (Rom. 8:11)

The resurrection of Jesus Christ is of tremendous importance to believers as we anticipate the future, because it is not only the guarantee, but it is also the model of our resurrection.

On the day of Jesus' resurrection, there were many believers who were also resurrected and appeared in Jerusalem (Matt. 27:52). They came up out of the tombs, went into Jerusalem and knocked on the doors of their family members. Jesus's resurrection accomplishes the resurrection foretold in Ezekiel 37, the story of the valley of the dry bones.[8] Additionally, the believers who were actually raised out of their tombs are a foretaste of our resurrection on the last day. As Jesus's body was quickened, so will ours be. As His body was glorified, so will ours be. These truths are important to the believer's expectation of rising from the dead.

5. The resurrection is the vindication of Christ.

The resurrection proved that Jesus is the Son of God. Jesus had offered the perfect sacrifice for sin, was found spotless, and was declared by God to be righteous in full. In that sense, it is impossible for the resurrection *not* to have happened. If the resurrection had not happened, the universe would have ceased to exist because, on the cross, God had poured out the fullness of His wrath on His sinless Son – the wrath that ought to have justly rested on a multitude of men and women, boys and girls because of their sin.

Fear Not!

Perhaps we have heard this so often during our lives that we have ceased to feel the wonder of it. But how can a just God pour out His wrath against sin on someone who is sinless? There are many answers to this question offered in the New Testament, one of which is that Jesus voluntarily became the substitute for sinners. He essentially said, "Lord, I'll stand in the place of My people. That is what I want to do, for Your glory and for their everlasting good. I want to stand in the place of the people that You have given to Me" (cf. John 10:7-18). Those beautiful phrases *for us … in our place*, which are found throughout the New Testament, are part of the way that the New Testament explains the wrath of God against sin being laid upon the sinless Son of God.

The New Testament also addresses this issue by saying that the Father vindicated Jesus by raising Him up from the dead; thus demonstrating to the watching world that Jesus did not deserve to die, because He was perfect in every way. Although Jesus did not deserve to die, He *did* deserve to be raised again from the dead. In fact, had God not raised Him from the dead, His justice would have been compromised.

Since God's justice would have been compromised had He not raised Jesus from the dead, then God's justice would also be compromised if He did not raise from the dead all those who have trusted in Jesus Christ, because Jesus died in their place. As a Christian, part of your firm and certain hope in the future resurrection is that it would be just as impossible for you not to be raised from the dead as it was for Jesus not to be raised from the dead, because He died in your stead. These truths about the resurrection are very comforting to us as believers.

What does Christ's resurrection mean for us when He returns?

A new question arises, about what Christ's resurrection will mean for us when He returns. Number 38 of *The Shorter Catechism* has such a beautiful outline of this that I thought we would start there:

Q. What benefits do believers receive from Christ at the resurrection?

A. At the resurrection, believers, being raised up in glory, shall be openly acknowledged and acquitted in the Day of Judgment, and made perfectly blessed in the full enjoying of God to all eternity.

The Shorter Catechism lists four benefits that belong to the believer upon death that are simply a summary of the Bible's teaching about what the resurrection of Jesus means for the believer on the last day.

1. Changed to glory.

First, at the final resurrection every believer will be raised, or changed, in glory. *The Catechism* puts it this way: "At the

Fear Not!

resurrection, believers, being raised up in glory...." This comforting truth comes from a number of different places, but one place in particular is 1 Corinthians 15:42-43:

> So it is with the resurrection of the dead. What is sown is perishable; what is raised is imperishable. It is sown in dishonor; it is raised in glory. It is sown in weakness; it is raised in power.

The apostle Paul is saying two very important things.

First, he is saying that just as you are buried in your body, so you will also be raised in your body. As Job would say, "Yet in *my* flesh I shall see God" (Job 19:26b). When that flesh – as weak and decaying as it is in this world – is raised, it will not be raised in weakness. The bodies of believers will be raised in beauty, immortality, and perfection. As we experience oppression in the flesh, it is comforting to know that we will see God in the flesh. Not only is that truth comforting, but as Thomas Vincent said, when we are raised, our bodies will be most healthful, strong, spiritual, incorruptible, immortal; they will be most beautiful, and glorious.

This is a very comforting reality. When I am watching dear saints who have trusted in Jesus Christ all their lives going through their final battle with some debilitating illness that has robbed them of the once robust capacities of their bodies, I love to remember that the next time I see those saints (in glory), not even a hint of that physical incapacity or infirmity will be present. The next time I see those saints, I will see them in heaven in the fullness of what it is and means to be created in the image of God.

When I see the children of believers who have been born with congenital and permanent disabilities of mind or of body, it is deeply comforting to know that when I see that child in glory, I will see her in the fullness of what a human being can be: no limitations, no incapacity, only glorified perfection.

Secondly, it is heartening to realize that our bodies will be perfected in the resurrection. When Christ comes again, and we are raised, our bodies will be raised in perfection – totally perfect, even as Jesus's body was glorified. You will not have one single physical deformity. You'll never struggle with being fat again – boy, am I looking forward to that! Your shoulder will never again give you trouble. Your lower back pain, your arthritis, your cancer will be no more. Your bodies will be like Jesus's glorious resurrected body.

Although there will not be a scintilla of imperfection in you, it is interesting that we are told in the Scriptures that there will be one mark that you will still see upon the body of your glorified Lord: the wounds that He bore for you. Jesus has kept the wounds in His glorified body, the wounds He received on our behalf. So for all eternity in your perfected body, you will be able to look at the body which the Lord has chosen to bear for everlasting time. You will gaze at the marks that He bore for you, so that you could inhabit a perfected body. It is a glorious thought, my friends, to think of what your Savior has done for you in that regard.

2. Acknowledged by Christ.
Every believer will in the final resurrection be acknowledged by Jesus Christ. Again, as *The Catechism* says: "At the resurrection, believers ... shall be openly acknowledged ... in the Day of Judgment...."

In Matthew 25:34, Jesus is telling His disciples what it is going to be like on that great day, and he says: "The King will say to those on his right, 'Come, you who are blessed by my Father, inherit the kingdom prepared for you from the foundation of the world."

On the last day Jesus is going to stand up and acknowledge His people publicly and personally as His friends, as His joint heirs, as His brothers or sisters. He is going to stand up before the nations and say, "These are My friends. I died for them. Everything that is Mine belongs to them." If you are a believer, then you will be publicly acknowledged, publicly embraced, publicly recognized, publicly owned, and publicly acquitted by Jesus Christ.

The blessing of this will be several-fold. We are told in the Bible that believers will be gathered from all the corners of the earth by angels (cf. Matt. 24:31). Won't that be a sight to see? After having been gathered by the angels (cf. Matt. 24:31), you will be placed at the right hand of Jesus Christ (cf. Matt. 25:33). At that point, we are told that Jesus Christ will openly acknowledge you as belonging to Him (cf. Matt. 10:32). You will then be entertained by Christ (cf. Luke 12:37) and invited by Him to take possession of His Father's inheritance, which He has purchased for you and given to you freely in His love (Matt. 25:34).

The apostle Paul adds that the Lord Jesus Christ will invite you to join Him in judging the world. In 1 Corinthians 6:2-3, Paul says that you will sit with Christ in judgment over wicked angels and human beings, and you will administer judgment with Him. Can you imagine that? Imagine the Lord Jesus saying, in effect, "What will be the just judgment that is meted out on this angel who rebelled against My Father eons ago? What will be the punishment that we mete out on these who so wickedly abused and oppressed people in this world? What does the judgment and justice of God call for?" In glory, you will administer justice with Christ and be publicly acknowledged by Him, acquitted by Him, owned by Him, embraced by Him, and recognized by Him.

3. Acquitted by Christ.
You will be pardoned and acquitted by Christ. Every believer will be in the final resurrection exonerated by Christ. The *Catechism* answers the question: "At the resurrection, believers ... shall be openly ... acquitted in the Day of Judgment."

Matthew 10:32 tells us that Jesus promises that "everyone who acknowledges me before men, I also will acknowledge before my Father who is in Heaven."

Before the watching world, on the Day of Judgment, there will be a public, absolute, universal, eternal acquittal of all those who rest and trust in Jesus Christ alone for salvation. Believers will be acquitted from false aspersions, which had been cast upon them in this life, but not only from all false accusations. They will also be acquitted from the actual guilt of the sins that have been committed by them in this life – acquitted because of the perfect obedience and satisfaction of Jesus Christ alone. In glory, you will be exonerated from every false charge that has ever been made against you, or that ever will be made against you in this life. But not only that, you will also be exonerated from every *true* charge that has been or ever will be brought against you in this life. Jesus Christ will publicly avow you as His.

Think of the eternal peace of conscience that will flow from this. Have you ever been so burdened by a false charge brought against you that you began to wonder whether it was true or not? You could not get it out of your heart or your mind. Or have you ever been so burdened by the reality of the guilt of what you actually have done, and the reality that there is nothing you can do to fix it? You can begin to wonder if you will ever get out from under such guilt. But the Bible teaches that if you rest and trust in Jesus Christ alone for salvation as He is offered in the gospel, on the last day Jesus will deal with both of those things definitively, so that you will never ever again lack peace of conscience.

4. Complete Happiness.

The Catechism says: "At the resurrection, believers ... shall be ... perfectly blessed in the full enjoying of God to all eternity." There are a number of beautiful Bible passages that speak of this, but three in particular stand out in my mind. The apostle John says,

> Beloved, we are God's children now, and what we will be has not yet appeared; but we know that when he appears we shall be like him, because we shall see him as he is. (1 John 3:2)

John in Revelation 21:4 reveals:

> He will wipe away every tear from their eyes, and death shall be no more, neither shall there be mourning nor crying nor pain anymore, for the former things have passed away.

1 Thessalonians 4:17 affirms, "So we will always be with the Lord."

At the final resurrection, every believer will be made completely happy in fellowship with God. This blessing of happiness and fellowship with God has two parts to it. First, we will be in perfect and final immunity from evil. In this world, there is no immunity from evil. Even the most precious of God's children suffers pain, trials, tribulations, and torments, but not then. This is precisely what John is saying in Revelation 21:4. God will wipe away every tear from their eyes. There will no longer be any death, no longer any mourning, no longer any crying, no longer any pain. All these things will have passed away. So the blessedness that we enjoy in fellowship with God is because all of the things that mar blessedness in this life are to be taken away permanently, finally, irreversibly.

Have you ever had one of those days that was so good that you began to fear it was never going to be like that again? You knew that something was going to happen, something was going to change. And it did. But never again will you face that in heaven. It will be perfection following perfection … following perfection … following perfection … forever.

There will not only be an immunity from that which mars our blessedness and happiness, but also a perfect enjoyment of God. John captures this thought beautifully in 1 John 3:2: "But we know that when he appears we shall be like him, because we shall see him as he is."

For the first time in our lives, we shall see Jesus as He really is, and it will take our breath away. And our breath will continue to be taken away for all eternity, because on earth we have seen through a mirror dimly, but there face to face (cf. 1 Cor. 13). John Owen eloquently captures this idea when he writes:

The queen of Sheba had heard much of Solomon and framed many great thoughts of his magnificence in her mind thereupon; but when she came and saw his glory, she was forced to confess that the one half of the truth had not been told her. We may suppose that we have here attained great knowledge, clear and high thoughts of God, but alas! When He shall bring us into his presence we shall cry out, "We never knew him as he is, the thousandth part of his glory, and perfection, and blessedness, never entered our hearts."[9]

Here we have known Him through His word, but we still wait to be transformed; we still live in this fallen, sinful world. But in heaven we will see Him as He is and so become like Him.

Don't you love how the apostle exhorts those Christians at the end of the first century by saying that "you love Him, though you have not seen Him"? On the Day of Judgment, that reality will completely pass away. Every last one of Jesus's children will have seen Him as He is. Even the disciples will have their breath taken away at the sight of Jesus when they see His glorified body, because they will be transformed into His likeness.

In that great day, there will be no one that we love more than Him. William Guthrie, the great Scottish pastor, said of Christ and the believer's sight of Him: "Less would not satisfy, but more could not be desired." Nothing less than Christ in His fullness can satisfy our God-given desires. After all, He made us to glorify and enjoy Him forever. Nothing less than beholding Him in all His fullness can enable us to glorify Him and enjoy Him forever. When we behold Him in the fullness of His beauty, our minds will not be able to conceive a thought of something greater to desire.

One of the old, Christian arguments for the existence of God was that "God is that than which nothing greater could be conceived."[10] It is a complex argument that I cannot fully address here, but the point is simply this: When we see Christ, all of us together will say, "There is nothing greater that I could conceive than Him. Nothing greater to delight. Nothing greater to satisfy." And so we will have a perfect enjoyment of God in Christ because we will see Him just as He is. That is what the resurrection means for us as believers.

What will the resurrected body be like?
The resurrected body of believers will be like Christ's body, glorious, perfect, and beautiful in every way.

When will the resurrection of our bodies occur?
When Jesus comes again, the resurrection of our bodies will occur.

Will non-believers be resurrected?
Yes, they most certainly will. Everyone will be resurrected. Those who have been resurrected trusting in Christ will be resurrected to be like Him and with Him forever. But those who do not believe in Him will be resurrected never to be like Him and never to be with Him for all eternity.

Our heavenly Father, it is hard for us to comprehend what Christ's grave-robbing, hell-defeating conquest of the death that we deserve and His life-giving resurrection mean for us, for it is so glorious. Grant that we would appreciate the fullness of the implications of His resurrection for us now, and then; and that we would live in light of that reality, day by day anticipating it, tasting it as the sweetest nectar that our lips could ever touch. Grant, O God, that You would give us a corresponding burden for those who do not love our Lord Jesus Christ, and who have grieved His heart of love. O God, we would have Paul's heart for his own people to the extent that he would have wished himself accursed if they could only taste and see that the Lord is good, if they could only trust in Jesus Christ. Give us that kind of love for those who don't know Jesus and do not love Him. Remind us that the resurrection is essential, necessary, part and parcel to the gospel, for without it we are of all men most miserable, and we ask these things in Jesus's name, Amen.

CHAPTER FOUR

The Final Judgment

He shall come not only in the glory of his Father, but in his own glory, as mediator: his first coming was under a black cloud of obscurity; his second will be in a bright cloud of glory.

Matthew Henry

The final judgment is one of the most maligned doctrines of our faith. "How could you possibly believe in something like that? That is just plain hard and harsh," people will often say. Well, friends, in light of the shooting incident that occurred at Virginia Tech; in light of what happened on September 11, 2001; in light of what happened at Columbine; in light of what happened at Nanjing, China; in light of what happened under Mao, under Stalin, under Lenin, and under Hitler there is no question as to whether it is right for there to be a Judgment Day. If there were no Judgment Day, God could not be right, because there is undeniable evil in this world that has not met a final accounting.

The doctrine of judgment is not a peripheral, harsh addendum that can be easily expunged from the Christian

Scriptures; instead, it is at the very heart of everything that God is doing, because it is God's purpose to see evil totally expunged from the moral universe of His joyful habitation. This is so that, for all eternity God, His righteous angels, His redeemed people, and our Lord Jesus Christ will never encounter evil again.

The Judgment Day is absolutely necessary. It is not some peripheral thing; it is not something drudged up from medieval memories stored deep in the recesses of our hearts. The Judgment Day is something that is clearly taught on the pages of Scripture. Along with the doctrine of hell, there is no doctrine that Jesus talked about more than that of final judgment.

As we seek to understand the Bible's teaching about final judgment, we will largely draw upon two texts, Matthew 24:29-31 and Matthew 25:31-46.

No man will be able to miss Jesus's return

Immediately after the tribulation of those days the sun will be darkened, and the moon will not give its light, and the stars will fall from heaven, and the powers of the heavens will be shaken. Then will appear in heaven the sign of the Son of Man, and then all the tribes of the earth will mourn, and they will see the Son of Man coming on the clouds of heaven with power and great glory. And he will send out his angels with a loud trumpet call, and they will gather his elect from the four winds, from one end of heaven to the other. (Matt. 24:29–31)

For hundreds of years, and especially in the last one hundred and seventy-five years, there have been various prophets, cults, and sects who have claimed that Jesus has come again, but somehow most of us simply missed it. The Bible, in contrast, clearly says that the sun and the moon will be darkened; the stars will be falling from the sky; and Jesus will be coming on clouds with glory before the watching world. Thus, there really is no reason to fear missing the second coming of the Lord Jesus Christ. Everyone will know of His return; it will be impossible to miss.

Jesus will return to establish the justice of God.

When the Son of Man comes in his glory, and all the angels with him, then he will sit on his glorious throne. Before him will be gathered all the nations, and he will separate people one from another as a shepherd separates the sheep from the goats. And he will place the sheep on his right, but the goats on the left. Then the King will say to those on his right, "Come, you who are blessed by my Father, inherit the kingdom prepared for you from the foundation of the world. For I was hungry and you gave me food, I was thirsty and you gave me drink, I was a stranger and you welcomed me, I was naked and you clothed me, I was sick and you visited me, I was in prison and you came to me."

Then the righteous will answer him, saying, "Lord, when did we see you hungry and feed you, or thirsty and give you drink? And when did we see you a stranger and welcome you, or naked and clothe you? And when did we see you sick or in prison and visit you?" And the King will answer them, "Truly, I say to you, as you did it to one of the least of these my brothers, you did it to me."

Then he will say to those on his left, "Depart from me, you cursed, into the eternal fire prepared for the devil and his angels. For I was hungry and you gave me no food, I was thirsty and you gave me no drink, I was a stranger and you did not welcome me, naked and you did not clothe me, sick and in prison and you did not visit me." Then they also will answer, saying, "Lord, when did we see you hungry or thirsty or a stranger or naked or sick or in prison, and did not minister to you?" Then he will answer them, saying, "Truly, I say to you, as you did not do it to one of the least of these, you did not do it to me." And these will go away into eternal punishment, but the righteous into eternal life. (Matt 25:31–46)

The Final Judgment will unmistakably demonstrate the justice of God. Throughout Scripture the words that are used of God's Final Judgment are words like *wrath, indignation, anger,* and *fury.* These are not words describing an out of control deity; instead, they are words describing the appropriate response of a righteous God to injustice, evil, and wickedness.

Believers often ask me about what the Judgment Day will be like for them, and honestly many of them tremble a little bit to think about it. But, for the believer, the Judgment Day will not only be a day of trembling. It will be primarily a day of vindication: a day of vindication for the believer; a day of vindication for Christ; and a day of vindication for God.

To better understand the Judgment Day we will ask several questions and answer them with the biblical data.

Who will be the judge?

Interestingly, in all Jewish literature leading up to the Gospels, God is pictured as the judge. The God of Abraham, Isaac, and Jacob is going to be the judge, and that is why it is so striking that Jesus identifies Himself as the judge. Matthew 25:31-32 says, "When the Son of Man comes ... then he will sit on his glorious throne ... and he will separate people one from another." Jesus is saying, in effect, "I am the judge. I am going to judge the nations." This is a clear testimony to the deity of Jesus Christ. He wants His disciples to know that He will judge the world. He is the King upon His throne.

Who will be judged?

The New Testament repeatedly states that the fallen angels, the angels that fell with Satan in the beginning, will be judged. Matthew 8:29, 2 Peter 2:4, and Jude 6 indicate that Satan and his assistants, the fallen angels or demons, will be judged.

Fear Not!

But Scripture also makes it clear that all human beings who have ever lived will together appear before the great white throne of judgment. The dead, both great and small, will all appear before the judgment seat; no one will be excluded. The wicked and the righteous, the great and the small, the quick and the dead will all appear before the judgment seat of God. Jesus makes this clear in Matthew 25:32 – "Before him will be gathered all the nations…" (see also Rom. 14:10 and in 2 Cor. 5:10).

Where does judgment take place?
The judgment will take place before the great white judgment throne. Where will that be? I simply do not know. But it will be before the Lord Jesus Christ on his throne.

What happens at the judgment?
The Bible teaches that there are a number of things that will happen on the final Judgment Day. So we will look at this question in multiple parts.

Separation
The first element on the Judgment Day will be separation. In Matthew 25, we are told that Jesus will divide or separate the world into two groups: the righteous and the wicked.

Have you ever heard Adrian Rogers talk about the list that was made in New York Harbor for the passengers who had been on board the *Titanic,* as they began to take account of those who had made it back? There were only two groups: the saved and the lost. That is exactly what Jesus says here. At the end of the day, we are not going to be red, yellow, black, or white; we are not going to be lower, lower-middle, middle, upper-middle, or upper class. There will be only two types of people, the righteous and the wicked. Jesus will separate everyone into these two groups.

Sentencing

Secondly, there will be adjudication. In other words, this final judgment of separating the world into two groups – those on the right hand and those on the left, the sheep and the goats, the righteous and the wicked – will not be an arbitrary separation. The separation will not be based upon whim; instead, it will be based upon deeds committed in the body. The entire life of each person, including the inmost thoughts and motives, will be brought into judgment. The basic decision, saved or damned, forgiven or condemned, will be rooted and grounded in justice, and everyone will have to admit, "This judgment was fair and right." Although the wicked will still hate God, they will have to acknowledge that the judgment is fair. Jesus's judgment will not be arbitrary; it will be utterly appropriate.

Revelation

Thirdly, in addition to separation and sentencing, there will be revelation in the final judgment. Scripture tells us that every deed a person has performed; every word he has spoken; every thought he has conceived; every ambition he has cherished; and every motive that has prompted him to action or to inaction will be laid bare.

Now before you run too far with this, let me say two things because this is one of the things that scares believers about the Last Day. Don't miss the point that Jesus is emphasizing here. In God's courtroom, there will never be one of those tragic miscarriages of justice that can occur even in the best legal systems of this earth.

Ever since we have uncovered so many uses of DNA evidence, we have occasionally found people who have been convicted by the legal system and later discovered that they were not the guilty party at all. There was no malice on the part of the prosecutors or on the part of the judge; they simply made a mistake. But Jesus wants you to know that the thoughts, the motives, the intentions, and the desires of the hearts of every human being will be opened up. There will not be any possibility of a mistake occurring in the Final Judgment.

Those of you who work in prison ministry find very often that 99.9 percent of the people in prisons are innocent! At least that is what they say. But after the judgment made by Jesus, when the heart has been opened before the world, no one – absolutely no one – will be able to make that claim. That is the first thing you need to understand. Jesus wants you to know that God's justice is going to be openly seen to be absolutely, scrupulously fair, just, right, and righteous; so that even those who hate the judgment that He delivers will have to say that the judgment was right.

Secondly, although the hearts of believers will be completely uncovered on the Last Day, it will all be done to the praise of His glorious grace. Your sin will be shown to the world, but it will redound to the praise of His glorious grace, and you will revel in the greatness of His grace to you despite all your sinfulness. Thus, there will be revelation on the Last Day (see Luke 12:3 and 1 Cor. 4:5). When John uses the image of books being opened, in Revelation 20:12, he is talking about the books of our lives being opened and read before the world. So, there will be separating, sentencing, and there will be revelation.

Explanation for the sentencing

There will also be a pronounced reason for the sentencing – we are going to see this when we come back to look at verses 34 and 36 of Matthew 25. There will be a sentence pronounced, and a reason given for the judgment being made. In other words, God will not simply say, "Guilty," and then move on to the next party. Instead, He will say, "Guilty, because of x, y, and z." Everyone in the world will see the reason for the sentence pronounced.

Execution of the sentence

There will also be an execution of the sentence on the Judgment Day. Jesus emphasizes this in Matthew 13. Verse 30 says:

Fear Not!

> Let both grow together until the harvest, and at harvest
> time I will tell the reapers, Gather the weeds first and bind
> them in bundles to be burned, but gather the wheat into
> my barn.

In other words, there will be a carrying out or execution of
the sentences that have been pronounced.

Vindication

This is the fundamental point of the Judgment Day. First,
God's justice will be vindicated. No one will be able to stand
up and say, "In my case You are not just. You have been unfair
to me." God's justice will be universally vindicated.

Secondly, Christ will be vindicated. All those who heaped
aspersions on Him, all those who denied and mocked Him,
will see Him vindicated before the whole world. Even the
damned will be obliged to admit in their inmost being that
Jesus is who He said He is, and that God is just.

Finally, God's people will be vindicated in that Day.
All those who rest and trust in Jesus Christ alone will be
vindicated in that Last Day.

The return of the Son of Man according to Jesus

Let us look at Matthew 25 again, in more detail, briefly
considering three things. Matthew 24 and 25 are prophetic
passages that deal with the end times – or to use the technical

term that theologians use, *eschatology*. Don't be impressed when somebody throws the word *eschatology* around. It simply means the study of the end times, or the study of the last things.

In Matthew 25:31–46, Jesus is giving you His conclusion to this great sermon on the last things, and He paints a picture of what is going to happen when the Son of Man comes.

In verses 31–33, you see the context or the setting of the final judgment. In verses 34–40, Jesus judges the righteous and their response is given. Then, in verses 41–46, Jesus judges the wicked and their response is given as well.

The context of the judgment

What if you were to stand before God on Judgment Day, and He asked you, "Why should I let you into heaven? Why should you be given the privilege of fellowshipping with Me forever? On what basis have you been made right with Me?" What would you say?

I hope that you would not say, "I tried to be a good person; I tried to live a good life; I've done more good things than bad things. I went to church two or three weeks out of every month. I was a deacon or served in Women's Guild." Instead, I hope that you would say, "My only hope in both life and death is in the precious blood of my Lord and Savior Jesus Christ, who lived and died for me. 'Nothing in my hand I bring; simply to Thy cross I cling.'"[11] I hope you will say, "I am trusting in Jesus Christ alone for salvation, as He is offered in the gospel, and it is my heart's deepest desire to fellowship with my Triune God forever. I know that I do not deserve it, but my Savior has redeemed me."

But what if God then said to you, "Well, what evidence is there that you trust in Christ for your salvation? What evidence is there that you are My child? What evidence is there that you really are a Christian? What evidence is there that real gospel grace resides in your heart?" What would you say then?

In this passage, Jesus is not teaching salvation by works, as some would like you to think. Instead, this passage has an irrefutable argument against salvation by works, while it also has a startling warning that we shall be judged according to our works. How do you put these two truths together? Your works do not save you, but you are judged according to them. How do you put those things together? Well, let us look briefly at this passage.

Jesus Is Judge of All
When Jesus comes again, He will come as the judge of all. Look at Matthew 25:31–33:

> When the Son of Man comes in his glory, and all the angels with him, then he will sit on his glorious throne. Before him will be gathered all the nations, and he will separate

people one from another as a shepherd separates the sheep from the goats. And he will place the sheep on his right, but the goats on the left.

There are three aspects to this picture: the majestic return of Jesus Christ with an entourage of angels in tow; second, the enthronement of Christ as a king with His assumption of the role of absolute judge; and then, thirdly, His actual judgment (or His distinguishing, or His separation) of the nations. This whole passage is designed to make it clear that Jesus is the very Son of God. Jesus is God. Jesus is divine. The metaphor used here of the judge as a shepherd comes right out of the Old Testament. Ezekiel 34:17 says: "As for you, my flock, thus says the Lord GOD: Behold, I judge between sheep and sheep, between rams and male goats." When Jesus comes and says He is going to judge and separate between the sheep and the goats, every Hebrew who hears this will immediately think of Ezekiel 34:17. Jesus is clearly claiming to be the Lord God of Israel. All of us need to come to grips with Jesus's claims to deity and to the nature of His second coming. He is coming as a king in judgment.

Jesus will judge all men and women
Who will be judged by King Jesus? In verse 32, it is evident that He will judge all peoples and all nations – every single

Fear Not!

person. The apostle Paul says in 2 Corinthians 5:10: "For we must all appear before the judgment seat of Christ, so that each one may receive what is due for what he has done in the body, whether good or evil."

As we have said before, that can be a scary reality even for the believer, but when the Christian looks up and sees that it is Jesus who is doing the judging, his heart will take comfort. In the Gospels, we are told that when Jesus died there were two thieves with whom He was crucified. At the beginning of the day, both of those thieves were mocking Him, but after a while, we are told that one of those thieves rebuked the other for maligning Jesus, and then said to Jesus, "Remember me when you come into your kingdom." And Jesus said to that guilty thief, "Today you will be with me in Paradise." When that thief stands before the awesome arraignment of God, he will look up and see the One who said to him, "Today you will be with me in Paradise." The sight of Jesus as the Judge – as awesome as it will be – will be the very thing that will give peace to the hearts of believers. My Savior; the One whom I love; the One who first loved me; the One who died for me – He is the One who is my judge. What comfort this will bring to the hearts of the redeemed. But unbelievers will tremble, because they rejected and neglected Him. When the Last Day comes, it will be far too late.

Jesus's judgment of the righteous and their response

In verses 34–40, King Jesus judges the righteous and records their response as He makes it clear that He shall reward those who trust in Him, and that His judgment shall be in accordance with their lives.

The people on Jesus's right, His chosen ones, are given a kingdom prepared for them before time. Since this kingdom was prepared for them before time, before the foundation of the world, it is evident that receiving the kingdom could not be based on their works.

In the passage, Jesus speaks to them about having cared for the hungry, thirsty, strangers, naked, those who were sick, and those who were in prison. Very often this passage is used to call upon Christians to show kindness to those who are in need. Such duties are non-negotiable aspects of the Christian faith. The Bible makes it clear from beginning to end that we ought to have a concern for those who are in need, but Jesus is not specifically talking about that here. In verse 40, he says, "Truly, I say to you, as you did it to one of the least of these my brothers, you did it to me." Jesus is saying that, at the end of time, judgment will be based on how you treated His followers.

When God told Abraham that he was going to be the father of the faithful in Genesis 12:1–3, He said to Abraham that in him all families of the earth would be blessed. But He also said to Abraham that those who bless Abraham, God will bless, and those who curse Abraham, God will curse. Jesus is basically saying the same thing in Matthew 25. Those who have blessed the people of God (who can bless the people of God but those who are the people of God?) will be vindicated. But those who curse the people of God (you cannot curse the body of Christ without cursing Christ) will be cursed. This shows us how inextricably linked Jesus Christ is to His people. When the apostle Paul was persecuting Christians in Jerusalem and then headed toward Damascus to persecute the church there, Jesus met him on the road, and said, "Saul, Saul, why are you persecuting me?" Jesus is so united to His people that when you persecute the church, you are persecuting the Lord Jesus Himself. And the opposite is true as well – when you serve the church, you are serving Jesus Christ Himself.

In Matthew 25, Jesus is saying that the judgment is going to be according to whether you blessed or cursed His body, His family, His people, the people for whom He died. This is not a passage about salvation by works, although it does make it clear that there is more to being a Christian than simply saying that you love and trust Jesus. There must be a life that goes along with truly professing Jesus Christ. This passage emphasizes that love towards other Christians, and especially those in extraordinary need for their labors in Christ, will be the measure and evidence of true love for Christ, and hence salvation. This passage does not teach that caring for the poor in general is the way that you are saved. If it does, we are all going to hell, because we could never possibly care enough. Instead, the good works performed by the sheep and not performed by the goats, though clearly related to the ultimate destiny of each group, are not stated to be the cause of their destinies. Instead, these good works are evidence of the true nature of these people.

Notice the response of the righteous. These believers are clearly not sitting around waiting to be justified by their works. When Jesus commends them for what they have done, they humbly respond by saying, "When did we do this?" That does not sound like folk who are waiting to be justified by works, waiting to be saved by works. Instead, they are completely stunned that Jesus would even mention their works.

These true believers love one another because of Christ's love for them. So, they were naturally doing that which pleases the Lord. On the Last Day, the Lord says to them in effect, "And by the way, your lives were beautiful to Me, because you loved one another. You did it not because you thought that you were earning your salvation, but because you were living in accord with the salvation by grace that I gave to you. By your love the whole world knows that you are My sheep."

Jesus's condemnation of the wicked in accordance with their lives
Those on the left, whether false believers or pagans or idolaters will be commanded to depart from God's presence;

will be sent to the same place of punishment created by God for His fallen angels; and will be condemned because of what they failed to do.

The condemnation here is not so much about what they did; instead, it is about what they did not do. That is a frightening thought, isn't it? Sins of omission are highlighted in the condemnation of those who are the goats on Jesus's left. The condemned failed to love lowly and needy Christians, and hence showed that they did not love Christ, irrespective of claims they might have made to the contrary. And here Jesus articulates the very uncomfortable and unpopular doctrine of eternal punishment.

Conclusion

Although salvation is by grace, true faith in Christ is always accompanied by a life of joyful, grateful service. We are not saved by that life. If that were the way of salvation, no one would be saved, because even the best of lives, no matter how beautiful they may be, are tainted with sin. The very best deeds that we have ever done are shot through with sin; nevertheless, the true believer always has a life that bears out faith; and the unbeliever always has a life that bears out disbelief.

In the final judgment, all will be definitively revealed. If we truly love the Lord Jesus, we shall live lives of love because of Christ's first love for us, but if we do not find ourselves living that life of love, we need to ask ourselves if we really love Christ at all. Have we truly trusted in Him and accepted Him by faith?

The only way to ever manifest love that is truly pleasing to the Lord is to trust in Jesus Christ alone for salvation. As Jesus said, in Matthew 7:16-20,

> You will recognize them by their fruits. Are grapes gathered from thornbushes, or figs from thistles? So, every healthy tree bears good fruit, but the diseased tree bears bad fruit. A healthy tree cannot bear bad fruit, nor can a diseased tree bear good fruit. Every tree that does not bear good fruit is cut down and thrown into the fire. Thus you will recognize them by their fruits.

Until we come to know salvation by free grace through Jesus Christ, we remain bad trees, bearing the fruit of sin and iniquity, piling up condemnation upon our heads. The Lord Jesus Christ alone can set us free from the power of sin to live such lives that are worthy of the gospel.

Father, our hearts do tremble when we think of the approaching Judgment, but we pray that we would live so that more and more we find comfort at the thought that at the Last Day the same One who died for our sins, the same One who reached out to us when we ourselves were down in the muck and mire of wickedness, will be sheltering our souls, and will declare us to be His friends, His brothers, His sheep, His children, His chosen. And we will share in His vindication, though we do not deserve it. And so all the glory will be His and Yours. Thank You, Jesus. Amen.

CHAPTER FIVE

What Is Heaven?

It is impossible for any creature to be happy without acting all for God. God Himself could not make him happy any other way. I long to be in Heaven, praising and glorifying God with the holy angels. All my desire is to glorify God. My heart goes to the burying place; it seems to me a desirable place. But oh, to glorify God! That is it; that is above all.

David Brainerd

On the night of His betrayal, Jesus was facing the dawning reality of bearing the full penalty of the sins of His people. As He was preparing for this unimaginable punishment, what do you suppose was on His mind? Jesus was thinking about heaven.

It is important for us to consider the reality of heaven not only in the face of great difficulty, but in our day-to-day lives. Jonathan Edwards made it his practice to meditate on heaven at least twenty minutes every day, and he often said that this gave him strength to live the Christian life. I wonder how many more of us would live hopeful and fruitful lives if our thoughts and meditations were more focused on the hope of heaven.

Comfort from Jesus

Toward the end of Jesus's ministry, the disciples are about to face a tremendous faith crisis – their whole world is going to collapse in the next twenty-four hours, and only Jesus knows it. The disciples are in the dark concerning the events that are about to take place, and so, as recounted in John 14, Jesus is trying to prepare them for it.

The disciples' impulse will be to look at the cross and think that something has gone wrong. "This should not be happening. Jesus should be being crowned King, not being crucified on a cross. Jesus should be running the Romans out of Israel and establishing again the kingdom of David. What has gone wrong?" But Jesus's whole message in the upper room to His disciples is that what happens to Him on the next day will not be an accident. It is according to His Father's design and Jesus's choice.

"Let not your hearts be troubled. Believe in God; believe also in me. In my Father's house are many rooms. If it were not so, would I have told you that I go to prepare a place for you? And if I go and prepare a place for you, I will come again and take you to myself, that where I am you may be also. And you know the way to where I am going." Thomas said to him, "Lord, we do not know where you are going. How can we know the way?" Jesus said to him, "I am the way, and the truth, and the life. No one comes to the Father except through me." (John 14:1-6)

Although Jesus was killed unlawfully, He was not "murdered" in the way that we normally use the word *murder*. When we speak about murder, we usually mean a victim who was at the mercy of an evil perpetrator. Jesus, however, is saying to His disciples that everything that happens to Him will be according to His choice and His Father's appointment. Not only that, but Jesus is telling His disciples that after the cross He is going to prepare a place for them that they might always be with Him.

Think of how comforted the disciples would have been if they only had understood what Jesus was saying to them. Think of how comforted you would be if you only understood what Jesus is saying to all who rest and trust in Him. Jesus's assurance to His disciples is not wishful thinking; it is one hundred percent true.

But Thomas blurts out, "We don't know where You're going, we don't know what You're talking about, and so of course we don't know how to get there!" Jesus's response is, "I am the way." It is similar to what He had said earlier (in John 11) to Martha: "I am the resurrection and the life." Jesus is focusing all their faith on Him, and by doing this He gives to them remarkably encouraging words. So, as we contemplate the reality of Heaven, let us begin with the very words of Jesus Christ.

Where is heaven?

The word "heaven" in Greek and in Hebrew has multiple meanings. In the Bible, it sometimes means "the sky," and so you will hear phrases like this: "The birds of the heavens …"

Fear Not!

This phrase simply refers to the birds that are in the sky. Sometimes the Bible says heaven or heavens when referring to the starry hosts, "the stars of heaven."

More applicable to our study, however, is what the Hebrews and early Christians called "the third heaven." The third heaven, or the heaven of heavens, is the place of God's abode. The apostle Paul makes reference to this when he is confronting the Corinthians who were thinking pretty highly of themselves spiritually.

> I must go on boasting. Though there is nothing to be gained by it, I will go on to visions and revelations of the Lord. I know a man in Christ who fourteen years ago was caught up to the third heaven – whether in the body or out of the body I do not know, God knows. And I know that this man was caught up into paradise – whether in the body or out of the body I do not know, God knows – and he heard things that cannot be told, which man may not utter. (2 Cor. 12:1-4)

The Bible uses multiple pictures and words to describe the third heaven. In John 14:2, "the heaven of heavens" or "the third heaven" is the place where God dwells, and Jesus describes it as "the Father's house." Jesus is telling His disciples that the third heaven, the place where He is going, is their Father's house. Now we could spend a great deal of time thinking only about that single truth, but I must simply return to Isaac Watts's paraphrase of the twenty-third Psalm:

There would I find a settled rest,
While others go and come;
Not as a stranger, or a guest,
But like a child at home."

In 2 Corinthians 12, Paul refers to heaven as paradise, and you can find this same terminology used in Luke 23:43 and Revelation 2:7. It is also called the "heavenly Jerusalem" in Galatians 4:26, Hebrews 12:22, and in Revelation 3:12. The Heaven of heavens, the place of God's abode, is called the heavenly Jerusalem. It is called "the eternal kingdom" in 2 Peter 1:11. It is called "the eternal inheritance" in both Hebrews 9:15 and in 1 Peter 1:4. In Hebrews 11:14 and 16, the third Heaven is called "a homeland" and "a better country."

In heaven, we are told that we shall also "sit at table down with Abraham, Isaac, and Jacob"; "be in Abraham's bosom"; "reign with Christ"; and "rest in heaven" (see Matt. 8:11; Luke 16:22; 2 Tim. 2:12; and Heb. 4:10-11).

The Bible describes heaven with beautiful and stirring imagery, but these truths only begin to scratch the surface of what heaven will really be like. In heaven, the blessedness that we enjoy will consist of the righteous possessing life everlasting (2 Cor. 4:17) and the exemption from evil that will be ours for all eternity. Never again will we be in the society of the wicked (2 Tim. 4:18), and there will be endless bliss and fullness of joy forever.

Fear Not!

Heaven is not only a state of blessedness, it is also a place that Christ has prepared. It is appropriate, therefore, to think of Heaven as a place – though it could mislead us if we are not careful. In the Bible, heaven is a spatial reality. It is a place. It can be located. Where is heaven? It is where Christ is, at the right hand of the Father. Where is that? That is where heaven is!

Obviously there are questions about heaven that I cannot answer, but the big question, I can answer. What we need to know about heaven is not so much where it is, but who is there. Heaven is where my Savior is. Heaven is where the One who has saved me and the One in whom I delight dwells. Therefore, I really do not care where heaven is located, as long as I am there with Him and with all of those who love Him.

What is heaven like?
The Bible teaches us to infer from various things in this life what the reality of heaven will be like. First of all, from the less than perfect relationships we experience with God and with others, the Bible teaches us to extrapolate from those experiences a perfect relationship free from limitations, frustrations, and failure. For instance, let's go back to the picture of the Father's house. For many of you that very image will bring back some of the most precious and treasured remembrances of your entire life, memories of

being at home with your father. My father died in 1992, and the world has never been the same for me. In some ways, I feel lost in this world, and the thought of being back in his house is one of the most delightful thoughts that I can conceive. Well, the Bible asks us to extrapolate from such less than perfect experiences to the perfect experience of being in our Father's house.

But for some of you, the memories of your father's house are not good. If that has been your experience, I have some good news for you. All you must do is extrapolate in reverse. In every way that dwelling in your father's house fell short of blessedness, your Father's house in heaven will not. It will be everything that you always longed for, but never experienced. So the Bible asks us to think about our earthly experience of fellowship with the Father, Son, and Holy Spirit, with believers in Christ, and with our experience in this beautifully created but fallen world, and extrapolate from that to our experience of God in heaven.

Secondly, the Bible asks us to think about our life, and eliminate from it all the forms of pain, evil, conflict, and distress that we experience on earth, and then think, "That is what heaven is going to be like." Revelation 21:4 explicitly does this when it says, "He will wipe away every tear from their eyes, and death shall be no more, neither shall there be mourning, nor crying nor pain any more, for the former things have passed away."

Fear Not!

John is telling you to think of a world with no sin, no tears, no sorrow, no betrayal, no disappointment, no failure, no rebellion, and no death, and that is what heaven is going to be like. As you begin to meditate on these beautiful truths, you will continually come back and say to the Lord, "Lord, I cannot imagine being eternally free from sin, because I have never even known a moment of such blessedness." Although we cannot experientially relate to such perfection and blessedness, Scripture reminds us to believe and hope in it, because we are going to one day know a world that contains no sin whatsoever. We are going to know a world where there is no suffering, no sorrow, and no death. The Bible continually asks us to think about our life now lived for God, but with all the forms of pain, evil, conflict, and distress of this life removed.

Thirdly, the Bible asks us to enrich our thoughts of heaven by adding every conception of excellence and God-given enjoyment that we now know and experience. In Revelation 7:13-17, John the apostle tells us:

> Then one of the elders addressed me, saying, "Who are these, clothed in white robes, and from where have they come?" I said to him, "Sir, you know." And he said to me, "These are the ones coming out of the great tribulation. They have washed their robes and made them white in the blood of the Lamb. Therefore they are before the throne of God, and serve him day and night in his temple; and he

who sits on the throne will shelter them with his presence. They shall hunger no more, neither thirst anymore; the sun shall not strike them, nor any scorching heat. For the Lamb in the midst of the throne will be their shepherd, and he will guide them to springs of living water, and God will wipe away every tear from their eyes."

These verses appear on the bottom of a monument in a graveyard in Edinburgh, Scotland, that was erected to honor 18,000 Presbyterians who were killed by their government from 1660 to 1688, because of their quest for religious freedom. Eighteen thousand! Many of their bodies were dumped into this common grave over which the monument was erected. John's words have become an eternal reality through Jesus Christ for each and every last one of them. Does that not comfort you, beloved of the Lord!

In heaven the redeemed will have no pain ... only joy
As we contemplate the excellency and the greatest God-given enjoyments we possess in this life, let me zero in on three aspects of the constant joy of life in heaven for the redeemed.

First, in heaven our greatest joy will be that we have a vision of God in the face of Jesus Christ. Peter talks about the fact that though we have not seen Him, yet we love Him. Though you and I have not seen the Lord Jesus Christ, we love Him. But when we arrive in heaven, we will see Him face to face. One day we will behold Him as He is. We will see Him in His fullness. Beholding our risen Lord will be the greatest joy of heaven (see Rev. 22:4).

Second, we will have great joy in heaven when we benefit from the on-going experience of Christ's love as He ministers to His people. Luke 12:37 says:

> Blessed are those servants whom the master finds awake when he comes. Truly, I say to you, he will dress himself for service and have them recline at table, and he will come and serve them.

When was the last time that happened? It was during the "Lord's Supper." In the upper room, Jesus took off His outer garments, girded Himself as a slave, and washed His disciples' feet. At the marriage supper of the Lamb, your Lord and Savior is going to gird Himself and have you recline at His table, and He is going to serve you.

When one of my professors read Luke 12:37, he could not believe what he was reading, so he went to his dear friend, Wilbur Wallace, who was a professor of New Testament at Covenant Theological Seminary in St. Louis. My professor said to him, "Dr. Wallace! Does this mean that Jesus is going to serve you and me?" To which Dr. Wallace simply said, "Bob, did you ever think that there would be a time when you didn't need Jesus to serve you?"

So for all of you who have known the ministry of Christ in this world during your deepest hour of need, you can simply think beyond that blessed reality to the greatness of the blessing of your Savior in perfection, serving you again at His wedding feast. It is not my word that is reassuring you of this; it is the Word of God that assures you of this fact. This is not some speculation; these are the words of Jesus Christ to you, His disciples.

Thirdly, the Bible makes it clear that our fellowship with loved ones and the whole body of the redeemed will be without reservation. Frequently, I am asked, "Will I know my loved ones?" My reply is, "Emphatically, yes!" Although the redeemed will be given a glorified body, the Scriptures give every indication that no matter what the shape of that glorified body might take; we will definitely know one another. You are familiar with the questions we frequently ask, "Will I be thirty? Will I still have my double chin? Will I still be about eight suit sizes too large?" Well, I honestly have no idea! Little children that go to be with the Lord, how old are they going to be in Heaven? Aged saints, who go to be with the Lord, what is their glorified body going to be like?" I simply do not know, but I can tell you beyond the shadow of a doubt that it is going to be better than you could possibly imagine. The resurrected body will far exceed even your wildest dreams, but we shall definitely know one another. Think of Moses and Elijah on the Mount of Transfiguration. Neither of these men had lost their identity; they were still Moses and Elijah. Your loved ones that have

Fear Not!

gone to be with the Lord, those whom you dearly miss, you will see them and know who they are. But they will not be as they were; instead, you will behold them in the fullness of what they have become through the Lord Jesus Christ!

In heaven there is a mediator ... In hell there is no mediator

Although we have already spoken about the horrors of hell, there is perhaps one more thing we need to say. It is a surprising thing to note, because so often we speak of hell as a place where God is not. Let me, however, say something provocative. Hell is eternity in the presence of God without a mediator. Heaven is eternity in the presence of God, with a mediator. Hell is eternity in the presence of God, being fully conscious of the just, holy, righteous, good, kind, and loving Father's disapproval of your rebellion and wickedness. Heaven, on the other hand, is dwelling in the conscious awareness of your holy and righteous Father, but doing so through a mediator who died in your place, the One who absorbed the fullness of the penalty of your sin. Heaven is eternity in the presence of God with the One who totally eradicated sin from your life, the Lord Jesus Christ.

Hell is eternity in the presence of God without a mediator. Heaven is eternity in the presence of God with a mediator, the Lord Jesus Christ.

ENDNOTES

[1]There is no question that the issue of the status, especially of the very young, is one of the most emotionally fraught and experientially intense questions relating to death that we can possibly encounter; and so, obviously, when we speak about it, we need to speak with great pastoral and personal sensitivity, especially when we are talking to somebody who is in their own experience wrestling with these issues.

Let me say a couple of things. Over the course of time, there have been those that have tried to address this question by arguing that there was an age of accountability before which you reach you are considered innocent, and therefore a candidate for heaven. The idea that there is some particular age in the course of normal childhood before which all children would be saved because they are not yet accountable for their sin is absolutely unfounded.

Biblically, the age of accountability is conception. David says, "I was conceived in sin." In Adam, we all fell, and so when I was born into this world I was born a sinner. That didn't happen when I got to be six or seven or eight. Going the route of trying to find an age before which you are not accountable and after which you are accountable is neither helpful nor biblical.

Secondly, let me say that most Christians have had, over the course of history, two views of this issue. They have either believed, with theologians like Charles Hodge and B. B. Warfield, two outstanding Presbyterian theologians, that in fact all infants are elect—the infants of believers and unbelievers—and that therefore all in infancy who die go to heaven. C.H. Spurgeon also held to that view. The arguments made for this view are complex, because there is not a lot of biblical data to help you in this area.

The other major view (that has been articulated by theologians like O. Palmer Robertson, who grew up at First Presbyterian Church, Jackson) is that the only positive assurance we can give is that the children of believers who die in their infancy are saved and go to heaven, because of the covenant promises of God given to believers and their children. Both of these groups of Christians would appeal to passages like the story of the death of David's illegitimate child by Bathsheba.

When David had his adulterous affair with Bathsheba, a child was conceived and born, but it was very sickly. While the child was alive, David covered himself with sackcloth and ashes, fasted, and prayed day and night that the child would live. But the minute the child died, he stopped fasting; cleaned himself up; adorned himself with his best clothes; anointed himself with oil; and went about his business. His friends were baffled by this. They were expecting David to react in a very different way. They expected him to fast and mourn once the child was dead. Instead, David said in response, "He will not come again to me, but I will go to him." Now some have said that David was merely saying that the child is not going to come back from the dead, but that David was going to die one day, too.

Fear Not!

The problem is that such an understanding of David's statement does not sound very comforting to me. I cannot imagine that view explaining David's actions at all. Instead, I think what David is saying (and most Christians have believed that this is what David was saying) is that he anticipates a reunion with that infant child in the life hereafter. This assurance enabled David to move on, as it were, upon the death of his child. And so again Presbyterians, among most Christians, have held one of those two views.

[2] Douglas MacMillan was a well-known pastor in Scotland in the twentieth century.

[3] Donald MacLeod is Principal of the Free Church College, Edinburgh.

[4] John Macleod, "Between a Hard Place and Satan's Spandau (Or, Why I Believe in Hell," Glasgow Herald, April 8, 1992.

[5] Ibid.

[6] Physical, bodily resurrection is the only kind of resurrection that the apostle Paul ever talked about. The idea of a nonphysical resurrection, which is present in some circles, is an utter anomaly with Paul.

[7] Paul was a Pharisee, and so the doctrine of a final resurrection would not have been problematic for him even prior to his conversion. The Pharisees did, however, try to cover up the resurrection of Jesus Christ, so even among the Pharisees there would have been serious doubt and disbelief concerning the resurrection of the Lord Jesus Christ (cf. Matthew 27: 62-66; 28:11-15). But the point being made here is that Paul needed no argument at all to convince him of the reality of the resurrection after his conversion, because he had beheld the resurrected Lord Jesus Christ with his own two eyes.

[8] In this passage, Ezekiel is shown this valley full of dry bones, which come back to life by the power of God.

[9] John Owen, The Works of John Owen, Of the Mortification of Sins in Believers, Etc., vol. 6, William H. Goold ed. (Edinburgh: The Banner of Truth Trust, Seventh printing 2000) 65.

[10] Anselm, Proslogion.

[11] Excerpt from Augustus Toplady's hymn "Rock of Ages."